DAVID ARCHULETA

Mitchell Lane
PUBLISHERS

P.O. Box 196
Hockessin, Delaware 19707
Visit us on the web: www.mitchelllane.com
Comments? email us: mitchelllane@mitchelllane.com

Mitchell Lane
PUBLISHERS

Printing   1   2   3   4   5   6   7   8   9

A Robbie Reader
Contemporary Biography

Abigail Breslin	Albert Pujols	Alex Rodriguez
Aly and AJ	Amanda Bynes	Ashley Tisdale
Brenda Song	Brittany Murphy	Charles Schulz
Dakota Fanning	Dale Earnhardt Jr.	David Archuleta
Demi Lovato	Donovan McNabb	Drake Bell & Josh Peck
Dr. Seuss	Dwayne "The Rock" Johnson	Dylan & Cole Sprouse
Eli Manning	Emily Osment	Hilary Duff
Jaden Smith	Jamie Lynn Spears	Jesse McCartney
Jimmie Johnson	Johnny Gruelle	Jonas Brothers
Jordin Sparks	LeBron James	Mia Hamm
Miley Cyrus	Miranda Cosgrove	Raven-Symone
Selena Gomez	Shaquille O'Neal	Story of Harley-Davidson
Syd Hoff	Tiki Barber	Tom Brady
Tony Hawk		

Library of Congress Cataloging-in-Publication Data
Scholl, Elizabeth J.
  David Archuleta / by Elizabeth Scholl.
    p. cm. — (A Robbie reader)
  Includes bibliographical references and index.
  ISBN 978-1-58415-758-8 (library bound)
  1. Archuleta, David—Juvenile literature. 2. Singers—United States—Biography—Juvenile literature. I. Title.
  ML3930.A73S35 2010
  782.42164092—dc22
  [B]
                                                                      2009004526

ABOUT THE AUTHOR: Elizabeth Scholl is a writer of books and magazine articles for children and young adults. A native of New York City, she grew up among a family of music lovers, listening to a mix of jazz, classical, and popular music. As an adult, Elizabeth enjoys many types of music, including pop, rock, and R & B, as well as folk and traditional music from around the world. When not writing, she loves going to see live music in New York City whenever she can. Elizabeth lives in Northern New Jersey with her husband and three children.

PUBLISHER'S NOTE: The following story has been thoroughly researched and to the best of our knowledge represents a true story. While every possible effort has been made to ensure accuracy, the publisher will not assume liability for damages caused by inaccuracies in the data, and makes no warranty on the accuracy of the information contained herein. This story has not been authorized or endorsed by David Archuleta.

PLB

TABLE OF CONTENTS

Words in **bold** type can be found in the glossary.

David Archuleta has always loved singing and expressing himself through his music. He got his chance to share his talent on *American Idol*.

A Golden Ticket

The summer after his second year of high school, sixteen-year old David Archuleta had a job working in a local park. When **auditions** (aw-DIH-shunz) for the TV show *American Idol* were announced, his friends told him he should try out. They knew he was a great singer and believed he was good enough to get on the show.

David's hometown of Murray, Utah, was far from San Diego, California, where the auditions were being held. It would cost a lot of money to fly to San Diego, and to stay in a hotel. David would have to quit his job to go. What if he did all that and didn't make it?

When his parents actually offered to take him to the audition, David decided he would go. He didn't know how far he would get, but he knew it would be an **experience** (ik-SPEE-ree-uns) he might never have again.

Arriving at Qualcomm (KWAL-kom) Stadium in San Diego, David got in line with thousands of other people hoping to be chosen

Jeff Archuleta plays an active role in his son's musical career. He explains, "Because I'm also a musician, I'm a little more involved. I'm like David's music consultant; someone he can bounce ideas off."

for *American Idol.* Everyone was practicing their songs, and David thought many of the singers sounded great. He thought he probably wouldn't make it past the first round of auditions.

When it was David's turn, he was asked to sing in front of two judges for only about 20 seconds. Halfway through his song, the judges asked him to sing something else. They liked what they heard. When David was invited to return for a second round of auditions, he felt like one of the lucky children in the movie *Willy Wonka and the Chocolate Factory.* He told *Life Story* magazine that he said to himself, "I made it! I have a golden ticket!"

David made it through more rounds of auditions in front of the *American Idol* **producers** (proh-DOO-surz), during which many people were **eliminated** (ee-LIH-mih-nay-ted). Every time David saw people being sent home, he was sure he would be the next to go. Instead, he was chosen to sing in front of the famous *American Idol* TV judges, Simon Cowell, Paula Abdul, and Randy Jackson.

David and his mother, Lupe Archuleta, had backstage passes at the Richard Rogers Theater on Broadway, where they had watched a performance of the hit musical *In the Heights*. The two have always shared a love of show music.

Rising Star

David James Archuleta was born in Miami, Florida, on December 28, 1990. His father, Jeff, is a jazz trumpet player, and his mother, Lupe, is a pop singer. She is from Honduras (hon-DOOR-us), a Spanish-speaking country in Central America. Some of David's earliest memories are of his dad playing his trumpet and his mom singing, in English and in Spanish. David is the second oldest of five children. His sister, Claudia, is a year older than he, and his brother Daniel and sisters Jazzy and Amber are younger.

When David was six, the Archuletas moved from Florida to the Salt Lake City area of Utah. David remembers his dad putting

Though David grew up listening to music and singing, it wasn't until he performed on *American Idol* that he discovered the power of music. "Music has the power to change how you feel," David believes. "That's what it does for me, and I'm sure it does for a lot of other people."

on a video of the musical *Les Miserables* (lay miz-ur-AHB) for David, his brother, and sisters while his dad and mom unpacked into their new home. David loved the music so much, he learned all the songs and walked around the house singing them. He sometimes even dressed up like the characters in *Les Miserables* and performed the songs in his basement. David recalled in his interview with *Life Story*, "That is when I started finding an interest in music. I started liking it on my own, and it wasn't just, 'All right, I'll listen to whatever you're listening to.' "

When David was twelve, he performed on television for the first time. *Star Search* was a talent show on which people competed in singing, dancing, and comedy acts. Like *American Idol*, if a **contestant** (kun-TES-tunt) won, he or she was invited to come back the next week. David returned again and again, until he became Junior Singer Star, winning the grand prize of $100,000.

Just when it seemed as if David's singing career was beginning, he had a major setback.

A year after he won *Star Search*, he was barely able to sing. Doctors told him he had **vocal cord paralysis** (VOH-kul kord puh-RAL-uh-sis). The muscles in his throat would not work properly.

For a while, David stopped singing altogether. His voice returned, but because of

David checks his hair after an *American Idol* episode. While he used to feel awkward about being in front of a camera, and still describes himself as "so weird-looking," he has gotten more comfortable with being himself. David thanks a friend who always brought a camera along and took pictures, which helped him get used to being photographed.

Even under the stress of the competition, David and his friend, *Idol* finalist Syesha Mercado, find a few minutes to be silly while warming up before the show. David shows off his healed vocal cords, while Syesha makes a face she probably didn't use in front of the judges.

the paralysis, it sounds a little different than it did before. David's vocal coach, Dean Kaelin, told the *Daily Herald* on May 18, 2008, "Some singers have something that gives their voice a **unique** [yoo-NEEK] quality, and this has done that for David."

13

David was introduced as David "Babyface" Archuleta, competing against David "Sugarface" Cook, on the final night of the *American Idol* Season 7 competition, described as "The Battle of the Davids." Though Cook walked away as the winner, David's singing was some of his best ever. Judge Paula Abdul told him, "It's like you're on fire tonight. It's pure magic."

American Idol

As David got ready to sing in front of the *American Idol* judges for the first time, he prepared himself to hear them say **critical** (KRIH-tih-kul) things about him. After all, as David said, "That's what they're known for." The judges surprised him by saying good things. Even Simon Cowell, the judge who is well known for saying unkind things about contestants, described David as "the one to beat."

Each week, David had to choose, learn, and practice a song in time for the show. There were so many other things to do to prepare for the show that once David had chosen a song, he had very little time to rehearse it. He went to American Idol School for contestants under eighteen, where he worked daily with tutors. He was also busy with interviews and having photos taken. He even was in a television commercial for Guitar Hero video game, and another one for DoSomething.org, a disaster relief foundation.

When David was chosen as one of the Top 24 *American Idol* contestants, he told *Fox News* on February 13, "It's amazing to make it this far . . . finally to the 24, it's just awesome. It's so cool."

Of course, David made it way past the Top 24. *American Idol* finally came down to two Davids—David Archuleta and David Cook. While it might seem like the two would dislike each other because they were **opponents** (uh-POH-nents), they had actually become close friends.

The final show was staged to look like a boxing match, with the Davids wearing boxing gloves and robes. Instead of a fight, the two finalists had nothing but compliments for one another. "As far as I'm concerned," David Cook

The Davids continue to be friends, and describe themselves as being like brothers. The two spent a summer on tour, along with the other *American Idol* finalists, and appeared together on TV talk shows. Their CDs even came out within one week of each other.

said, "the competition's over, and we're just having fun."

When Cook was named the *American Idol* winner, David Archuleta, the runner-up, said, "I think Cook deserved to win more than anybody."

Utah Governor Jon Huntsman, Jr., greets David on May 9, 2008—David Archuleta Day. David's day was filled with appearances, interviews, and visits with family and friends, and concluded with David singing the national anthem at the Utah Jazz basketball game.

Family, Friends, and Fans

David's family supported him even while he was in Hollywood and they were home in Utah. In his "exit interview" at the end of Season 7, David told AOL Television, "My whole family has been such a great support and they're the ones who have kept me grounded and allowed me to be who I am today."

David is also grateful for his friends from his hometown of Murray. Friends say David is shy when you first meet him, but when you get to know him, he is really funny. He is very polite, and was a good student when he was in high school. David used to run cross-country, and likes to in-line skate, but there is nothing he does that means as much to him as music.

CHAPTER FOUR

His good friend Mietra says, "Music is David's life and always has been."

In fact, several friends say David loves music so much, he will start singing any time

Hometown fans honored David by carving his image into a cornfield at the 13th Annual Cornbelly's Corn Maze and Pumpkin Fest. The maze, which covered 12 acres, included the phrases "Archuleta 4 President" and "Utah's Idol."

people are talking about something that makes him think of a song. He has a lucky charm that is a rubber band his friends gave him. It reminds him that they always have his back, which means they will always be there for him.

David's fans live all around the world. Some fans call themselves Arch Angels, and some call themselves Archies, because of the nickname "Archie" that David was given by fellow contestants on *American Idol*. Perhaps some of David's biggest fans are those from his home state of Utah, who showed David how much he is loved on May 9, 2008. The governor of Utah declared that day David Archuleta Day. According to *The Deseret News*, David said to his fans, "It means the world to me that you guys came here. I can't believe it. It's crazy. I can't thank you guys enough." David was so touched, he was moved to tears.

David performs at the Q102 Jingle Ball 2008 at the Susquehanna Bank Center in Camden, New Jersey. The audience went wild over his version of the song "Have Yourself a Merry Little Christmas." The Jingle Ball was just one stop in a whirlwind of post-*Idol* touring.

David Gives Back

Just a few weeks after *American Idol* season 7 ended, David and the other finalists began the American Idols Live! Tour. They spent the summer performing in front of thousands of fans around the United States. David told *TV Guide*, "We're all on that stage together again, but we're not competing against each other."

While David was on the American Idols Live! Tour, his first single, "Crush," was released. It immediately became a hit, selling over a million copies. The song came from David's CD, *David Archuleta*, which was released in November. It quickly went gold, selling over 500,000 copies.

David sings with *American Idol* finalists Carly Smithson, David Cook, and Brooke White at the Idol Gives Back concert. They were joined by other celebrities, including Miley Cyrus, Snoop Dogg, and NFL players Eli and Peyton Manning. The money raised would help organizations fight diseases such as AIDS and malaria, provide medical care for children, and help hurricane victims in New Orleans.

24

David has used his fame and some of the money he has earned to help others, especially children in need. He sang on Idol Gives Back, a concert to raise money for poor children around the world. He also helped by answering phones when people called to donate money.

An exceptional moment in David's life occurred when he visited a girl in San Diego who is fighting cancer. Make-A-Wish, a group that helps "make a wish come true" for very sick children, arranged his visit. "It was probably one of the most special things I have ever experienced, and incredibly touching," David wrote about his visit.

David's charity work has inspired many of his fans to help others as well. A group of fans called Crush Kids Cancer–David Archuleta's Angels raised over $47,000 for a charity called Stand Up to Cancer.

Music is probably the greatest way David gives to others. He told *Life Story*, "Sharing something that you love to do with other people, and the fact that they can feel the same thing that you can feel through the music is one of the best feelings you can ever have in life."

As for the future, David has thought about becoming an ear, nose, and throat doctor. That way he could help people with conditions like the vocal cord paralysis he had. For now, though, he is enjoying being able to touch people with his music. David hopes he will be able to keep singing and making a career in

David performs at the Holiday of Hope Christmas tree lighting in December 2008. The event helped raise money for One Heartland, an organization that helps children affected by HIV/AIDS.

Things don't seem to be slowing down for David. In April 2009, he sang a duet with Miley Cyrus on *Hannah Montana,* and he was scheduled to tour with singer Demi Lovato that summer.

the pop music world. This hope is shared by the many who have been won over by David's strong voice and gentle personality. Although he was voted the runner-up, for David's fans, he is a real American idol.

27

CHRONOLOGY

1990 David Archuleta is born in Miami, Florida, on December 28.

1997 David and his family move to Salt Lake City, Utah, in February.

2001 David sings for the first time in public at the Utah Talent Competition; he wins the Child Division.

2003 David appears on and wins the television talent competition *Star Search*.

2007 David auditions for *American Idol* on July 30.

2008 David Archuleta Day is declared by the governor of Utah and is celebrated in David's hometown of Murray, Utah, on May 9. David wins second place on May 21. Along with the other *American Idol* finalists, David begins the American Idols Live! Tour on July 1. His first single, "Crush," is released on August 12. He wins a Teen Choice Award for "Most Fanatic Fans" on August 3. His first album, *David Archuleta*, is released on November 11. He sings at the Macy's Thanksgiving Day Parade in New York on November 27.

2009 David makes his acting debut on Nickelodeon's TV show *iCarly* on February 7. He appears on *Hannah Montana* and sings "I Wanna Know You" with Miley Cyrus.

DISCOGRAPHY

Singles

2009 "I Wanna Know You" (with Miley Cyrus)
  "A Little Too Not Over You"

2008 "Crush"

Albums

2008 *David Archuleta*

FIND OUT MORE

Books and Magazine Articles

If you enjoyed this book about David Archuleta, you might also enjoy the following Robbie Reader Contemporary Biographies from Mitchell Lane Publishers:

Ashley Tisdale
Demi Lovato
Dylan and Cole Sprouse
Miley Cyrus

Miranda Cosgrove
Raven-Symoné
Selena Gomez

Works Consulted

Adair, Aly. "David Archuleta, Utah's *American Idol* Hopeful, Shares His Life Stories." April 29, 2008. http://www.associatedcontent.com/article/741623/david_archuleta_utahs_american_idol.html?cat=7.

Adler, Shawn. "*American Idol* Front-Runner David Archuleta: Where Did He Come From?" MTV, March 4, 2008. http://www.mtv.com/news/articles/1582685/20080303/index.jhtml.

FIND OUT MORE

"David Archuleta: In His Own Words." *Life Story*. Bauer Publishing Company, 2008.

Dreben, Jed. "David Archuleta: End of Idol is a Big Relief." *People*. May 22, 2008.

Fletcher, Lisa, et al. "Behind the Big Voice: Who Is David Archuleta?" *ABC News*, April 2, 2008. http://abcnews.go.com/print?id=4572812.

Jensen, Maurine. "David Archuleta Makes His Mark on *American Idol*." *Meridian*. May 22, 2008.

Molyneux, Logan. "And the Winner Is David . . ." Daily Herald, May 18, 2008. http://www.heraldextra.com/content/view/266764/136/.

Pierce, Scott, and Nicole Warburton. "David Mania: Thousands Turn Out to Salute Archuleta." *Deseret News*, May 10, 2008.

Rancilio, Alicia. "David Archuleta Singer Still Adjusting to the Limelight." *Daily Freeman*, December 27, 2008. http://www.dailyfreeman.com/articles/2008/12/27/life/doc49557265464bd490865803.prt.

On the Internet

The American Idol Website www.americanidol.com

"David Archuleta: Biography." David Archuleta Web. http://david-archuleta.org/x/?page_id=77

David's My Space page www.myspace.com/davidarchuleta

The Official David Archuleta Online Community and Website www.davidarchuleta.com

GLOSSARY

audition (aw-DIH-shun)—To sing, dance, or act to try to get a part in a show.

contestant (kun-TES-tunt)—Someone who takes part in a contest.

critical (KRIH-tih-kul)—Likely to find fault with others.

eliminated (ee-LIH-mih-nay-ted)—Removed.

experience (ik-SPEE-ree-uns)—An event someone lives through.

opponents (uh-POH-nents)—People who compete against one another.

producers (proh-DOO-surz)—People in charge of making a show.

unique (yoo-NEEK)—Not like any other.

vocal cord paralysis (VOH-kul kord puh-RAL-uh-sis)—When one or both of the muscles that allow you to speak, called vocal cords, don't open or close properly.

INDEX